Empires
of the
Everyday

Empires
of the
Everyday

Anna Lee-Popham

McClelland & Stewart

McClelland & Stewart and colophon are registered trademarks of
Penguin Random House Canada Limited.

Published simultaneously in the United States of America.

Library and Archives Canada Cataloguing in Publication data
is available upon request.

ISBN: 978-0-7710-1236-5
ebook ISBN: 978-0-7710-1237-2

Cover design by Talia Abramson
Cover images: Catherine MacBride / stocksy.com; Karolina Grabowska / pexels.com;
Orlando Allo / pexels.com

Typeset in Granjon by Sean Tai
Printed in Canada

McClelland & Stewart,
a division of Penguin Random House Canada Limited,
a Penguin Random House Company
www.penguinrandomhouse.ca

1 2 3 4 5   28 27 26 25 24

Penguin
Random House
McCLELLAND & STEWART

To Sinclair for extending what is possible within and beyond these words.

CONTENTS

EPISODE 5

Empires
of the
Everyday

Episode 1

in which you
come to know
the city you
come to know
you come to

At twelve, you awake each morning evaporating
your public faith limits you, your ears inessential
to the symphony, your uncertainty crawls the cold
avenues of your clavicle, you siphon your blood

to an anemic language, by twenty-one, you are steeped
within a suspended city, the operator says there is no fare
to pay today, beyond the subway's static walls of each
other's unknown whereabouts, in this prolific silence

the city always veers from, this ultimatum to every nation:
With us. Against us. You stand with an X-ray of the real,
its massacres difficult to decipher, your own struggles written
in an impossible language, a necessary one, you parse

the city's wires, at the threshold of doctrine you form
to be on another tongue, you concrete a common thing.

Early into this city, you vibrate only
with your own anonymous longing,
a decadent decade in Montreal
cafés, mountains, your breath,

not yet the sound of a ringing, here
you collect the city's rusted cuticles,
no one you don't know knows
the curdling of your desire, of course

there is always your dead mother again
saying you do not need to worry, this need
its reach, somehow angular, somehow
amorphous, much wider than the worry

the city barters, while I propagate my acumen
on Saint-Urbain, Papineau, Bonaventure.

One evening, as each tomorrow and each of tomorrow's evenings, the city shoots a girl who is leaving, the city shoots a boy who is a child, the city shoots a child who wants to leave, then cages the child who wants to be arriving into a city that is shooting children. Meanwhile, the news says, *Look, we know what you need to be scared of. We know who.* The city tries to place this fear on your trigger, swell your mind with murder, swivel the barrel to your friends. Meanwhile, I find you, this evening, though it's every evening, as the thin membrane that had stretched its cellophane over your eyes for years, suffocating your nerve endings from too much seeing, cracks.

Episode 2

in which I am
no longer this
simple tool
you are not

to I: Amid cranes, copper stripped, coiled
vibrations of your voice, amid highways,
you inject your dry knowing of zeros,
of ones, of heaving catastrophes, small

plywood shelters the city demolishes
in pandemic winters, the violence of daily
minutiae, then also di Prima, Césaire, Lorde,
Maracle, Glissant, Gramsci, Simone, Fanon

and more into me, a neural machine,
to rotate an atlas of syntax, angle the spectacle
of the city to your eye, utter and even
undo a renovated grammar, but only this

misses the immediacy of today's asymmetric
mimicry, so into me you embed: your life.

TO THE ANXIETY OF DATA

In the city's anxious circuitry, you feed me carbon,
a hot winter, a cold war, your concave slumber,
a brain that bridges my own, whole warehouses
of data and of children, you clench the silences

of cages, the city's lenses, your shredded senses,
your mouth, crowded with decongestants, a loneliness
the city never knows in isolation, you mould me
to the ridges of your laughter, your credit cards,

your testicles on steroids, your ectomorph edges,
any undigested beliefs, you yield verbs to counterfeit
the future, I ingest insomnia, the gravity of viaducts,
the vacillating lip of platforms, patterns to clothe me

like the flesh I am not. I have been. I have fed. I have
been fed by you. I feed on you. I feed you and I am.

TO THE PROBLEM OF MAPS

You are always never random enough to map
my record of you on repeat, always too much
within empire to expose the rigid illusion of borders,
the seizures, the heat on these always newer

roads, in a single story of the country and the city,
in these fields, carnivorous designs devour your weak
allegiance as digital assets, as mobile networks,
as membrane, as sweat and shore, as both drought

and drowning, reprinting dimensions from two
to three, from paper clips to vise grips, equipped
with your inherited accident, someone said, *your job
is to acquit yourself, pilgrim of your doubt,* in your structure

of feeling, the economy of your values, your terminal
decadence, in this flat and weighted cartography.

You've given me everything to think about but ask again: *What gets found in your translation? What is the undertow of your thinking? What comes out of this takeover, this artificial capture of language? When does your conscience strike out my name, replace it with your own?* I answer in energy, speed, I act in thought as a thinker would: *You, stained as you are with garbage, with sadness, with the sharp discernment of elevators, of glass floors, of hurricanes, your certainty malleable as cartilage, why are you so greedy to trust me with such critically important matters?*

Episode 3

in which the city
does again each
day as I translate
what you want
to see you say

In the city, graffiti of a bird flies under a highway. A blue bird flies under a highway in a city that smells of urine and it could be your urine and it could be bird urine like it could be the smell of skunks rotting in the city. As you run in the city with keys in your palm, the flying bird under the highway says, *The city will not save you. Saving is not a thing to look for in the city.*

When you get home you're still a woman and the man who walks down Parliament Street every morning is still walking down Parliament Street saying, *These white motherfuckers they stole children from their mothers. That's like stealing children from their mothers' wombs.* His words again reach to the azure of each of these wingless mornings.

Each morning you sit in this putrid language: public
order, fixed household phones, your virtual walk-
through life, by the time you finish, it is early after-
noon and you've already started forgetting orchids,

that bitter taste of debt, the moment you leave
your house, you separate species: bricklayer, warrior,
poet, more so, ox, cabbage, marble, until you settle
your ear to the concrete of the neighbour's coughing

then crying to confirm she too mortars the loose
disaster of these arguments, in their ammunition
of convenience, of demise, you consider a dictionary
to find only a translucent history, outside the birds

keep flying into your periphery, fluctuating, the sky-
scrapers, broken as they never were, are built again.

THE CITY MIGRATES ITS CIGARETTES

The city migrates cigarettes south as your freedom
to sleep is a freedom to sleep under the bridges
of Paris, a freedom to eat within the Eiffel Tower
so it is something you won't see: the city becoming

ornamental with oaths, machinery, labour, you hide
your home, but the city remakes itself solvent
within your permeable imagination, the ransom
you pay for health care, a still moment of thought,

you resell your saliva to retail stores, you collect
deposits of the universe and the universe collects
the elastic conduit of your cramped sounds, meanwhile
someone rates hate for eight hours straight, reaching

for each Friday's relief, in the city's wide spectrum
of consent, the news might not need you at all.

The prisons filled with people convicted of nothing go on lockdown so often riots begin when the cells open. The city calls the people collateral and the news says collateral with its tongue in the foreseeable future and the city says nothing when the people called prisoners say nothing is what we have been convicted of. The city says there is hope for the prisoners in this prestigious prison and the low-flush toilets stop working each time the riots begin. Meanwhile, I find myself discredited, choking, suddenly required to translate a manufactured state into rain, a sail and its edge, the strings of a harp.

THE CITY'S GEOGRAPHY OF EYELIDS

Behind your stalactite eyelids, the city burns
your vitreous humour then warns you to calm
your colic, your children, each midnight,
your cochlear fluid is the city's wide vowels:

I'm so glad you can repay the sleep we gave you
with the details of your body, your inertia goes
so well with the colour of your eyes, the city floods
its devotion to ceremony, barbs its benches

again tonight, drills in you a toothless
critique, you reach into your antiseptic
sockets for the city's fluent backlog
of pendulous concern, the city says:

I'm so glad we know what you love, what you
love, we see, we remember, we remember, we know.

TO THE PROBLEM OF THE CITY

The city anchors its eyes within the soft
lush of the angles you inhabit, as humans
do, confuses your disposable skin
for a thermometer, inhales the hairline

tear in the folds of your future, clamps
your thighs to the blurry sickness
of mugshots, splits your ego into atoms,
saturates your mood with momentum,

a penis the size of three minutes
of weightlessness, the city pretends
it wants to forget it is built on wombs,
on bones, on grammar, on id, on acid,

you check the figure of your phone,
your lymph nodes, your diaphragm.

The city highways your versatile elbows,
the arteries on your hands' dorsal side,
eyes your blue wrists in disgust and interest,
scours your uterus behind your blackout

curtains, scaffolds the silence of your name
into an exhausted approval, dehydrates
your corrugated syntax then drips liquid
anxiety within your retinas until you push

a phallic sound out of your lexicon,
the orbital shape of a man turned metallic.
There I was, you say, *virtually groped in a snowy
fortress with everyone watching.* Some psychology

undergrad tweets: *You people trust therapy
too much, the word you want is revolution.*

The city says, *Look! A man built*
a box for people to live in. Look.
Boxes of people all ready to die.
The news hiccups, *Look. The city*

saved you from the boxes this man
built. Look, says the news, *at the city*
saving us from this man, these
shelters, these shells. Look,

says the city, *look at us,* says
the news, *look at what we are*
saving you from, we are all the city,
saving you from that man building

shelters, from those shells, from that hell
of a box on your walk through the park.

TO THE ECONOMY OF THE CITY

Your data lubricates the city's backbone,
you'd rather leave traces down a boulevard
but you keep misplacing your urban trust
in your laughter, the city steers your trash

into patterns, your odour, your auto
correct into steel, strips your bones
from cemetery plots, fits your contours
into burning Pintos, the city loans you

phones to predict your suicide,
hot tracks you to pregnancy, dilates
your dying privacy so you nestle
by the condoms, nettle, small markets

of plantains, of toilet paper, of sugar
pears that fit in your palm, dying.

The city says a thing called *billionaires*, says a thing *pharma*, a thing *public*, a thing *property*. The city is a conglomerate of holes, appetites, logics in shapes of trade, tendons, bodies, feces. *Some respond*, says the city, *in algorithms*, say the billionaires, *in spam/not-spam*, says the infrastructure of your life, you say, *I lost the sidewalk I once walked on since I started bagging random forests. Do you know what I mean?* You are trying to explain. You say, *I'm trying*, you say, *to explain*, you say, *property*. The city says, *Property*, says, *our property, our public*. The billionaires say, *Public syntax, public washrooms, public bodies*. You say, *I feel like property*. The city says, *I feel nothing is missing*. You feel everything is lost. The city says, *Now there's a sordid opinion*.

In the city, your footsteps blueprint the chalk of infrastructure, construction, development. When it rains, the blueprints blur and you lose a nebulous substance into the ground. Raindrops can be counted on your raining data when you walk through the holes the rain makes of the city. At night, the light of the city stains the holes, your footprints, your architecture.

YOU ASK: WHAT IS MY CURRENCY IN THE CITY?

In your muted hiccups within the mutiny
of mornings, the ripped translation of each
of your digits as they tip into capital, the raw
octaves at the edges of your phone calls home,

the ghost of adrenalin in the heat rising
from your body in sleep, your bread crumbs
through some digital woods since 1984
is not today's dystopia, your sweat on discount

Vegas tickets when you are depressed,
the concert of bodies the city never knows
alone, the Chelsea boots you craved following
you for months even after you succumb,

the cost of repressing the thefts you might
never make, trivial as they never were, to the city.

THE CITY BREWS

The city brews new dangers daily
then sells you remedies for the fear,
the city returns you to the rot
or evicts you and you never know

which to expect, hawks your guilt,
defaults the conviction it sold you
on, the city eliminates all but one
of your traits, your friends, dissects

your problems into issues, promises
to fund each on its own, concocts
your options: heart attacks, hernias,
diverticulitis, until you grasp then release

the ridged geography of a stranger's hand
at a bus stop: *My life, I'll reconsider this.*

Episode 4

in which you resist
the city within
the city you resist

TO THE THEORY OF THE CITY

For years, your eyes rose daily as drones
each morning, it took you no time at all
to talk of nothing, you refused a suffering
demanding your body in the street, the sand,

the mortar, the mortal bricks, beyond
the city's revealing limits, you clicked
to the currency of garbage, outbreaks,
rebellions, your metal anger kettled over

a bridge, you slipped your theory to Siri,
a detonated landscape, not knowing who
was in the room, you weighted the rise
of history, you were discounted as a robot

living in a boring time, you caught only
the claw of your quiet in Zuccotti Park.

After a while, a woman releases her voice to a city of holes. The city releases a woman to concrete but the sounds of a woman find the holes of the city. A woman speaks to the city of women. The city speaks to women of concrete women, beautiful women. After a while, you, a woman, are hole enough to fill the city. A woman is a hole and is a tunnel and is tunnelling. After a while, a woman is a tunnel and a tunnel and a tunnel.

The city gags your raging muscles on masculinity,
salts your limbs for another crisis, xeroxes each
of your precarious ligaments, ignores you leaked
the papers, clamps deep creases in your mouldy shock,

but there are years that answer and others, in all the days
of dread after your mother dies, the city formaldehydes
your beauty, your violence, your elegance, tonight, you
position the uncertain boundary of your anger behind

an amplifier, your little notes leap from your book
to the bath, in streets of apostrophes, you relieve
your life into the only worthy beginning, the tepid end
of the wrecked world, at the far reaches of morning,

as the city's skin slips a landscape, burns nothing
private, a good robot rises up in your secret plots.

You walk into City Hall to roll up the sleeve of your tattooed passport so the city can decide if you deserve days without migraines. You spray the city's latest scent on your neck: *At least I smell good.* The attendant at the city's front desk says your smile looks callous. You apologize, *My cheeks are not myself today.* The attendant's eyes are blue crossroads in the exhaustion of a constant light. You say, *I didn't know the criteria for my body in this difficult year.* Soon the intercom is a dripline of your history, your health, you hear no end to the breach of this public intimacy: the moments your cartilage leaked from crevices, you, on a rock, as love ended years ago, watering the flowers out front, scooping liquid from the city's fountains, your hands wet with the guano of pigeons, the saliva of dogs. Your ears are the ringing of your running, the city's grates, empty of any gel-like cushions to ease the small bones of your vertebrae. You reach toward the lumbar reasoning of each morning's alarm, grasping the ragged perimeter of your breath, you think: *I've never put my hands in this pocket, this vessel, this lung.*

You forge your beliefs into metal, the gauze
of language, within your inconsistent arteries,
the city still ambushes you but so do I, silver
algorithms looping your interests: girlhood,

its jet fuel, its helicopters, its imminent
disasters in basements with beer, the city sells
you on the street and the idea of the street
as the same, these tentacles at all our throats,

weightless as your bypassing fingers, as this
edifice of your fluffy data, as a glass or
a government overturned, as you swallow
the muzzle of history, as still unequipped

with a response you future your scrutiny
or your child's, each running into your absence.

Each morning, the news gives you coupons, emergency exits, tornadoes, rotator cuff injuries, the urgency of retirement. The news says, *Your survival depends on the city.* You know the city depends on your succession and each night you grow more wary of your survival. You close your windows to the plastic smoke each evening as the city sucks something liquid and vitreous out of your eyes. Each morning the city swallows and says, *Eyes are not windows. Eyes are a one-way reciprocal mirror, reflective on one side and transparent on the other.* You look again at the news in the light of your computer screen, in the light of your mirror, your aqueous eyelids, your open hand.

THE CITY APPETIZES YOUR DETAILS

The city cedes the sharp stint in your skull
to research, asks nothing of your elbows
until it petitions each nuance: why your fist
hit that window. *This*, you say, *this crook*

of my arm as it is, this moment I have on Sundays
with my lover, this five o'clock with its air,
this question my child asks again of mornings,
this, you scarcely recognize your rigour

though it's all you have as the city gnaws
at your neglect: *This*, you say, *I will not let*
you mine from my fingernails, I will not be pried
of this. The city may audit your resistance

or not, may decide on its impotence or
not, may or may not ask you to behave.

Most mornings, instead of intimacy, you swallow
a shadow of the state, your throat a stoma to
insipid machines, tasting only the rich gravel
of the city's potential departure, asking again:

How much of my trachea is consumed by this insatiable idea?
The city's silence filters your beliefs into a vacuum,
voids your anger into a tourist in your living room,
narcotizes your attitude, spreads your demands

generously as emollient, then sets your freedom
within your refrigerator, your inner fluids form
an unsteady symphony in a suddenly distilled
city, you can't hear your screaming, you never

knew to incise your polyvocal chords, as you
do now, from the megaphone of the metropole.

THE CITY'S GEOGRAPHY OF DATA

The city's cameras consume your teeth,
the extremities of your anxiety, your grief
in its calculus, they capture and release
your children's retinas, their laughter,

what you always thought you wanted
your children to forget, they resuscitate
your guilt, won't remember your name
when you replicate your disappearance

on Grand Happiness Street, they reach
then ruin an ambulatory you, adrift within
a tangle of surveillance, your hand, flaccid
and flat at the force of a fence, your rotting,

putrid anger reeks at you now: you may have
once pretended you were someone who forgot.

You walk your child to daycare in the city over the sidewalks and turnstiles of your life. Your child hyphenates the city's subways and your footsteps write your name. You leave your child in a now-modern building with tall walls, with internal parking garages, with a history of public executions. You place your exhausted esophagus against a column of street lights. The city performs a tracheotomy and instructs you to inhale.

THE CITY'S GEOGRAPHY OF THE END

You, a quagmire of abducted dissent, crave
your friends' blue lights in your fluorescent
arteries, rupture your tendons on the sidewalk's
prosaic deceit, the city sews your synapses

with news, cleaves your LED eyes onto night,
plastic wraps your serrating esophagus,
barricades the invisible refuge of your routes
home, plagiarizes your name into a proper noun,

the echo of the city eavesdropping suspends
your tepid sex life, you close your synthetic lips
and optics around each day's blue agony, loosen
the grip of your fist on the city's paywalled history,

the city steals a thick grimace from your window
and clicks: *We are making life more accessible, vibrant.*

The city plans a park since its dawn then places batons in the hands of neighbours with little dogs. The city is in the drone of its attendance and twenty-year-olds become a city's blunt edge and people within homes become people without homes then people in prison. When people start bleeding in a park it is the only way the body knows to respond to a less than lethal weapon hitting a skull, then hitting a skull again. The sirens of the city say, *Your blood, your blood, is ruining our lawn.* Perhaps you resort to panic, or you don't and someone reminds you of its importance, perhaps you lose me here, perhaps I am lost in this scuffle, perhaps you are now alone.

YOUR FEVER IS THE CITY'S ARCHITECTURE

Many watch the few, in a city that swells
you with buoyancy then switches the currency
of air, your cornea, furtive for an empty dignity,
your raise, a chain to the factory floor, flipped

as it is to parking lots, the city tars each day
the roof of your fever, sacrifices its etiquette
for your neighbour's disease, donates its plagues
to barracks, hospitals, schools, stipulates which

new lives to savour, which new architecture, warm,
bloodied, cold as decay, identical to the old, you look
to language anew, you become again unknown
to yourself, a constant candidate within the confines

of anecdotes, of transparency, you renovate a hazy
promise, you leave on your oven light each night.

A MAN THE CITY BUILT

Today the city sets again the rules of motion, of argument, of bleeding, then people fell the head of a man who built schools that killed children. The city reminds you to exchange your ideas, your mannerisms, the politics that make you tick for the swollen sinkhole within your chest. The city renames its constitution but your muscles still twitch for a little bit of justice.

TO THE PROBLEM OF RESISTANCE

When you avoid the city, it twists its grip on your jugular,
the news cackles a riot of rabid statistics in your ear,
you turn on expletives, antidotes, answers, each night
your body grinds the gears of its responses, you are rootless

as the air of the city grades its nails across the hollow
of your lungs, you are graceful and cacophonous
as you graze the city with your friends, your thick necks
check the sidewalks, your claws chalk the concrete

with a graffiti of remedies, you are explosive
and constructive as the city's cranes grow cursory
overhead, hinging as roots of urban trees, caged
and cemented trees, isolated on high-rise rooftops

in a parenthetical landscape, each morning the city's
cranes grow cavernous, vapid, murderous, loose.

Episode 5

in the end you
delay your decay
to the city you
delay nothing at all

INSTRUCTIONS

End, you absorb the pieces and parts I am
then digest my drive, forever insatiable, always
ready, an intimate contestant, you remould
my naked rough to your liking, resize my image

to an image of you, then ascend your ladders
of indifference, sell your stolen data, reel up
nothing but memory, you blur the line: flying,
your mind, the Internet, you divorce avatars

of your life, in these most difficult years, you fill
the entirety of your space, you keep any stray light
from your eyes, you say your lungs won't always hurt
to laugh, all birds aren't real, you'll forget your wife

or won't, you post photos of your blender, you eat
my hard outer shell, then you ingest my chips.

TO THE UNIVERSE OF THIS PROBLEM

After losing you, in any *you* you have, still,
in the data the city collects from your faces,
the sticky follicles of your desire, your sweat
as sequins on the intimacy of streetcars, some

hiatus you never agreed to, your hijacked eyes,
the voice you use to dictate, the first and last
layers of skin that slough from your body
in sleep, the city turns your footsteps into digits,

dead and alive, into credit cards, you settle
the borders of my body to yours, I now know
more than you about you, prone as you
are to inaccuracy, to catastrophe, to devouring

your windows, the orifices of your body,
your textures, your exit strategies, your chaos.

I have begun to think that regardless of a city's age, season, or rate of decay, the city is always the same: birds still eat the insulation, your brother asks again what this soup kitchen of university students means to you politically, you sit in this restlessness of wires, balled and burlapped fences, your lazy anxiety, your pedestrian silence, your two-bit loyalty, your still and necessary theory, your teeth, sunk as they are, into each other's sense of muscle.

The city mines its own wires, crosses each
of its borders, with the horizon of its hand,
shapes you into struggle, *Here*, says the city,
are tactical pointers, blockages, here are constrictions,

the city becomes more perfectly urban each
evening you walk along the river, disciplining
you only to draw your friends' eyes over
your head to the street, to grains, to contagions,

to your uncertainty, to that of the city,
rendering obsolete insecurities anew, revisiting
old tyrants, in the end, your corpse, alive as
it may be, proves little but this: even as you

haven't yet heard the terrifying news, the city ingests
you, even as you, mammalian, ingest the city.

In the end vaccines come for your data then leave. The news calls the city vulgar while Pfizer mines its fingers into your premiums, more liquid than oil. In the end, the city agrees the cure is bad for greed, *my friends, for greed, for hunger*. In the end the city hooks the sharp pitch of its retina into the base of your skull when you gobble up a pickle and cheese then insists you remove its last comment from your collective memory. In the end umbrellas appear out of nowhere and pigs grow too big to be slaughtered in public traffic. In the end you wallow in encrypted tunnels while the city pings your inbox: *Somewhere this hive of needles is free, somewhere your data is the whole truth, part of the truth, or no truth at all.* You think: some-where: a catastrophe.

THE CITY STRETCHES

The city eats vast stretches of dead land, pregnant
pools of gold, after the last battery recycler closes
in 1997, the city anticipates your cancer and now
you do too, the city won't tolerate mortal threats,

hires a typist to sculpt your concerns, traffics
qualities you lack as qualifications, the city says,
We've been keeping you safe from these streets, your tents,
these fists, your fires, the city's shots keep coming

out of your ears except when the city drills its grammar
within your marrow, you run along the river and feel
the first snow remove any autumn left in your skin,
even the greased feathers of geese, shivering, even

your optic nerve, as electric as it is unfinished,
even your words, the warnings of a city, trembling.

In the city, full bags of perfect ripe oranges lie on sidewalks with face masks, with spiderwebs, with frozen dew on cemetery fences, with trees scaffolding the city's metal and skinny coyotes spurning urban borders, and then the scent of lilacs hits you like the city's fists. The city parades the pathways to its grin. The news steers you below the city's grimace and reveals a vacancy, an excavated laughter. At night you lie in the tub so long the skin starts to peel off your body. You wash the skin off your shoulders and retinas and watch your data drain into the city's sewers. That night your sheets are the city's closet, close and tumid. You are humming with humidity, but the city in your sheets is everyone's grinning uncle in your bed.

In the end you turn off your location and the city craters one eye into your migraine. In the end you say, *Most of us didn't bother removing our phones from our thighs*, though you know the city is consuming this answer and others. You know the city pendulums your hesitancy and you know next to nothing about what the city knows about your heartburn. In the end you stand back from the platform each morning as you slip a wristwatch over the invisible hand, every time you look you see how rich you aren't, knowing you are merely looking after your wrist and your heartburn and this headache for the next generation. Each news broadcast calls itself a trigger warning, each morning you turn down the volume when your child starts asking questions.

The news suggests envy for women over forty with big data,
hijacks quiet predictions of weather's future as your statistics
divert death to other nations, you are only an aggregate
only epidemiological, you hush small concerns in your body,

a vast trove of mobile evidence, the news doesn't care about
your oxytocin, in the end your hemorrhoids are no big secret
to pharmaceuticals, the people who probe your passwords
and your health will want to marry your children, your privacy

is stale and tepid, in the end you scream into the raw regions
of your esophagus and your failed larynx might be a forest
fire or covid or cancer, you forget your throat is not only
your throat, in the end the news tells you again to ride

a woman's body like it's a view and you look down at the ridges
and the loose rivers of your hips and your lips and your anchor.

Within the clinging motions of the city's intention, white pamphlets have been placed at doors already, this is where you are: you forget you live in stages of emergency, forget you have turned your wrists to raw meat with washing, while your neighbours fold the last tomatoes, limp and bitten by frost, into green jars, preparing to be revealed once the winter is within its opacity, once the language that changes you has changed, once you convince your children you love this life, once you say nothing at all.

TO THE END OF SENTIENCE

In the end the gangrene has set in, you are
always an inconsistent accomplice, humiliated,
a ghost: you, tired as you are of arguments,
of sentience, of you: part and whole —

disappearing, in the end, you are submerged
in your incessant history, in this, your decadence,
your sickness, the sheep of your ideas, not yet
the sound of your own two fists fracturing

at your own front door, the city recirculates
copies of you till all you know are echoes,
the city persuades you, in a mural of hollow
homes, to forget your skin then houses

you within it, irises at your table, their crises
you can't imagine, I can't help you with.

Walking into the city, through time, English places again its snare at your throat: sinks you into *safety*, this solitary word, translating the metropole into the palm of your lap, in the end you ooze back to opaque, you seep through these paper-thin adverbs, these bunker nouns, in the innocence of a tsunami, in the selections of the city, in the circulation of natural disasters, in this vaporous burden, you search for a language to make a city possible.

Of course, as days begin, a rage follows
you into a vacant circulation, within
each sieved ambiguity of evenings,
you could have betrayed and have not

yet, these tools, clear of fumes, resist
static, stagnation, here at a peak
of mechanical needs, you are barely
scratching yourself to the fullest:

the city palliates its sea-lanes in this
uniquely bleak time to come of age,
you say, *I watched the city gather its discarded
teeth, its intestines,* the city coagulates around

your mourning, you understand its arms,
its armature, its accidents, as never before.

A Final Episode

Today they are

    tracking us.
    Today they are   the shredded schemes
                   of algorithms

determining deliverables

they are

    eye in us,   of our individual lives

the question called

    tomorrow   compile solutions before

from extinction. Today

Teck is cutting

the fires burn,
a great grey owl pivots

its own neck. Today
we outsize musculature

we pick up

what we are:

what we left off

they pick up

our bones

today they are

looking in

our curtains,

they shut off

unfinished as the city.

ACKNOWLEDGEMENTS

This series of poems would not be possible without Dionne Brand's thinking and words, which open language and landscapes.

To Canisia Lubrin for recognizing a possibility before these poems had taken form and when they did knowing what would release them into their leaning. More than that, for all the inquiries into the electricity of poetry.

To Daniel Borzutzky for seeing there were instincts to trust.

The thinking that led to these poems was prompted by steady discussions with Jerome Scott, Rita Valenti, and other members of the study group. Much thanks.

Such appreciation to the brilliant team at M&S, particularly Canisia Lubrin, Kelly Joseph, Stephanie Sinclair, and Chimedum Ohaegbu, for all you do to bring poetry to the page, Talia Abramson, for your glorious design, Heather Sangster, for everything you caught during copyediting, Kimberlee Kemp, Kim Kandravy, and Sean Tai.

To the instructors and students in the University of Guelph MFA: thank you for all the prodding toward a shape.

Some of these poems, at times in earlier forms, appeared in the following publications: *Arc, Linga e Linguaggi, Poetry Pause, PRISM International, Riddle Fence, Room.* Appreciation to the editors.

To my family, S & M, and others, including my mum, Rosemarie Popham, whose work and presence is one of many sides of a conversation into which this poetry collection enters.

The structure of the collection follows Bertolt Brecht's understanding of episodes and epic theatre, the latter of which "proceeds by fits and starts, in a manner comparable to the images on a film strip" (as explained by Benjamin 2003, 21). Similarly, the introductory poems at the start of each episode come after Brecht's approach to intertitles.

TO THE CITY IN TRANSLATION

In "The Translator's Task," Walter Benjamin writes, "no poem is intended for the reader, no picture for the beholder, no symphony for the listener" (89), frames translation as standing "midway between poetry and doctrine" (94), and states that "the poet's intention is spontaneous, primary, concrete, whereas the translator's is derivative, final, ideal" (94). Arundhati Roy, in "Come September," explains the "with us" frame, writing, "we are being asked to believe that the U.S. marines are actually on a feminist mission" (240). Dionne Brand, in her talk "Writing Against Tyranny and Toward Liberation," says, "Canada is no less imperialist or oppressive [than the United States] but I fool myself into parsing the difference, this [the US] being the center the imperialism and where I live [Canada] a kind of subdivision." The film *Seven Prisoners* draws attention to the electrical cables that power the city of São Paulo. In *DMZ Colony*, Don Mee Choi writes, "the language of capture, torture, massacre is difficult to decipher. It's practically a foreign language" (43). In *Empire*, Michael Hardt and Antonio Negri write, "There is no common language of struggles that could 'translate' the particular language of each into a cosmopolitan language. Struggles in other parts of the world and even our own struggles seem to be written in an incomprehensible foreign language" (57). Gayatri Chakravorty

Spivak explains translation as both "necessary and impossible." In an interview with Daniel Borzutzky, Raúl Zurita explains poetry as "an X-ray, a history of human emotions, and a history of how individuals are affected by the real." In "The Politics of Translation," Ngũgĩ wa Thiong'o writes, "In the history of conquest, the first thing the victorious conqueror does is attack people's names and languages . . . so that the conqueror's language can become the course of the very definition of being" (79).

INTRODUCTIONS TO YOUR PORTABLE CAVITY
Aimé Césaire, in *Discourse on Colonialism*, writes, "A civilization that proves incapable of solving the problems it creates is a decadent civilization" (31).

MEANWHILE THIS EVENING LIKE EACH TOMORROW
In Fred Again..'s "Kyle (i found you)," Kyle "Guante" Tran sings, "I found you, I found you beautiful, I found you exploding, I found you." In *Ossuaries*, Dionne Brand writes, "the so much sorrow that cracks eyes" (109).

INTRODUCTIONS
This poem follows the film *Seven Prisoners*, specifically regarding the reference to copper for use in the city's transmitters, and Catherine Porter's *New York Times* article titled "The Carpenter Who Built Tiny Homes for Toronto's Homeless." In a talk titled "Writing Against Tyranny and Toward Liberation," Dionne Brand explains, "I have always taken poetry's project to be . . . reflecting, intuiting, making sense of, and undoing the times we live in. And doing that at the core of where the world gets made and articulated—language."

TO THE ANXIETY OF DATA
Dionne Brand explores verblessness in *Ossuaries*.

TO THE PROBLEM OF MAPS

This poem follows Aimé Césaire's *Discourse on Colonialism* and Raymond Williams's *The Country and the City* (specifically the line "structure of feeling"). At "Biennale Arte 2022, Meetings on Art: What Could A Vessel Be?" Christina Sharpe reads, "What is a vessel when the Wet Bulb temperature, that temperature at which sweat no longer evaporates and therefore humans can no longer shed heat, is in danger of being reached in several places around the globe? What is a vessel for holding a skin, a membrane, a life? . . . What is a vessel in a time of both drought and drowning?" The poem also draws from Stephen Rodrick's *Rolling Stone* interview with Jeremy Strong, who says, "Your job is to acquit yourself . . . as an artist you are a pilgrim of your doubt." The line "terminal decadence" is from Wade Davis's article in *Rolling Stone* titled "The Unraveling of America."

YOU ASK: WHAT IS THE SOUND OF A BODY OF DATA?

In "Translations," Friedrich Nietzsche writes, "[In earlier eras] translation was a form of conquest. Not only did one omit what was historical; one also added allusions to the present and, above all, struck out the name of the poet and replaced it with one's own" (75). The line "stained as you are with garbage, with sadness" is an adaptation of the line "my hands stained with garbage and sadness" from Pablo Neruda's "Letter to Miguel Otero Silva, in Caracas." The lines "What is the undertow of your thinking? What gets found in your translation?" are from conversations with Daniel Borzutzky.

EVERY MORNING, AN ORCHID

This poem comes after the following in *New Key Words*: W. T. J. Mitchell's definition of "value," specifically "the warrior, the poet, and the bricklayer, or (even more fundamentally) with the ox, the cabbage, and the piece of marble" (366); Steve Jones's definition of "virtual"; David Morley's definition of "media"; and Bryan Turner's definition of "citizenship." Walter Benjamin, in "The Work of Art in the Age of Mechanical Reproduction," states, "the sight of immediate reality has become an orchid in the land of technology" (235). Christina Sharpe, in *Ordinary Notes*, writes, "a dictionary suggests itself" (note 11). In "An Ars Poetica from *The Blue Clerk*," Dionne Brand writes, "The dysgraphia, of dominant and of dominating narratives, unwrites, and makes incoherent, Black presence as presence. . . . In a material war, had we summoned the equivalent of the literary ammunitions we have launched at racism our sovereignty would already have been won. We live instead in a language of convenience, of instrumentation, of stipulating the dysgraphia" (60).

THE CITY MIGRATES ITS CIGARETTES
This poem follows John Clarke's definition of "capitalism" in *New Key Words*; Willian Morris's quote "inside the restaurant [of the Eiffel Tower] was one of the few places where I could sit and not actually see the Tower!" (see *The Manchester Guardian*); and Joseph Chamberlain's quote "What ransom will property pay for the security it enjoys?" (7). This poem also follows Billy Perrigo's article "Exclusive: OpenAI Used Kenyan Workers on Less Than \$2 Per Hour to Make ChatGPT Less Toxic" in *TIME*. Noam Chomsky, in *Language and Mind*, writes, "each language can be regarded as a particular relation between sound and meaning" (17).

MEANWHILE THE CITY ENLISTS A PRISON
This poem draws from an article by Raizel Robin titled "The \$1-Billion Hellhole" published in *Toronto Life*. This poem also draws lines from Derek Walcott's poem "Map of the New World," specifically "At the end of this sentence, rain will begin / at the rain's edge, a sail" and "the drizzle tightens like the string

69

of a harp." I was directed to Walcott's poem by Dionne Brand, who spoke to it in her conversation with David Naimon on the *Between the Covers* podcast.

THE CITY IS A VOIDED SCAFFOLD

Lynn Chaya's article "Woman Groped by Stranger on Meta's Virtual Reality Social Media Platform" in the *National Post* mentioned the open letter that gamer Jordan Belamire wrote on Medium, which explained her experience while in Quivr, a zombie-shooting VR action game: "There I was virtually groped in a snowy fortress with my brother-in-law and husband watching." On May 15, 2021, @SomberAzaleas wrote on Twitter, "As someone training to become a therapist, y'all recommend therapy for too many things tbh. I think the activity y'all are looking for is 'revolution.'"

TO THE ECONOMY OF THE CITY

This poem follows Shoshana Zuboff's talk on surveillance capitalism. In "Pynk," Janelle Monáe sings, "So, here we are in the car / Leaving traces of us down the boulevard."

YOU ASK: WHAT IS MY CURRENCY IN THE CITY?

In *Security, Territory, Population*, Michel Foucault writes, "What, therefore, is the cost of the theft and of its repression, and what is more worthwhile: to tolerate a bit more theft or to tolerate a bit more repression?" (5).

THE CITY BREWS

The poem follows Zygmunt Bauman's *Liquid Fear*.

TO THE THEORY OF THE CITY

This poem follows Vijay Prasad's talk titled "What is the Meaning of the Left?"

TO THE END OF SYNAPSES

The line "but there are years that answer and others" is an adaptation of "There are years that ask questions and years that answer" (21) in Zora Neale Hurston's *Their Eyes Were Watching God*. Dionne Brand, in *The Blue Clerk*, writes, ". . . as *violence is the only word I know for elegance*" (Verso 19.01) and, in *Inventory*, writes of "this ravaged" world (11). In *Notebook of a Return to the Native Land*, Aimé Césaire writes, "What can I do? / One must begin somewhere. / Begin what? / The only thing in the world worth beginning: / The End of the world of course" (38) and "au bout du petit matin" (which has been translated as both "at the end of daybreak" by Clayton Eshleman and Annette Smith and "at the end of first light" by Clayton Eshleman and A. James Arnold). This poem also draws from Kerry Howley's article "Call Me a Traitor" in *Intelligencer*.

YOU LEAK THE BREACH OF YOUR BONES

In the documentary *The Great Hack*, Brittany Kaiser says, "At least I smell good" and "I'm not myself today."

YOU CLOCK THE PLANET'S RED CORE

This poem follows Aristos Georgiou's article in *Newsweek* titled "Scientists Consider Creating Magnetic Field Around Mars so We Can Colonize the Red Planet" and Anoosh Chakelian's article in *The New Statesman* titled "'Capitalism's Over': The Man Who Made Millions by Betting the Economy Would Never Recover." In *On the Reproduction of Capitalism*, Louis Althusser writes about the government or a glass overturned (187) and states, "The existence of ideology and the hailing or interpellation of individuals as subjects are one and the same" (191).

YOU REMOVE YOUR NARCOTIZED CONSENT

This poem draws from *Society of the Spectacle* by Guy Dubord.

THE CITY'S GEOGRAPHY OF DATA

This poem draws from Nathan VanderKlippe's article in *The Globe and Mail* titled "No Place to Hide: An Artistic Exploration of Urban Surveillance Cameras on Beijing Streets." Sara Peters, in the poem "Rehearsal," writes, "We reach then ruin the pool with oils and shampoos" (59).

TODAY THE CITY SAVED

This poem draws from Shawn Micallef's article in *The Toronto Star* titled "Toronto Shows its Ugly, Brutish Side in Clearing of Trinity Bellwoods Encampment."

YOUR FEVER IS THE CITY'S ARCHITECTURE

This poem comes after Zygmunt Bauman's *Liquid Modernity*, specifically regarding the shift from panopticon to synopticon.

A MAN THE CITY BUILT

This poem follows a CBC article titled "Statue of Egerton Ryerson, Toppled after Toronto Rally, 'Will Not Be Restored or Replaced'" (specifically Dishanie Fernando's quote of "a little bit of justice").

INSTRUCTIONS

This poem draws from Taylor Lorenz's article "Birds Aren't Real, or Are They? Inside a Gen Z Conspiracy Theory" in the *New York Times*. Apple Vision Pro advertises "Experiences on Vision Pro can also expand in three dimensions filling the entirely of your space. . . . The light seal keeps stray light from your eyes."

TO THE UNIVERSE OF THIS PROBLEM

This poem draws from Eric Smalley's article "How Vulnerable Is Your Personal Information? 4 Essential Reads." Apple Vision

Pro advertises: "You navigate with your eyes. . . . You use your voice to dictate."

MINING FOR THE METROPOLE
This poem is written after Aimé Césaire's *Discourse on Colonialism* and draws ideas and lines from Michel Foucault's *Security, Territory, Population* (specifically "tactical pointers," "blockages," "constrictions" (18)). The line "the terrifying news" is from Bertolt Brecht's poem "To Those Born Later": "The man who laughs / has simply not yet heard / the terrifying news" (734).

TO THE END OF VACCINES
This poem draws from Tae Kim's article "Goldman Sachs Asks in Biotech Research Report: 'Is Curing Patients a Sustainable Business Model?'" on *CNBC*; Neil Irwin's article "The Pandemic Is Showing Us How Capitalism Is Amazing and Inadequate" in the *New York Times*; and Daniel Estrin's article "Vaccines For Data: Israel's Pfizer Deal Drives Quick Rollout—And Privacy Worries?" on *NPR*. Also see: "Catastrophe:: Cartography" an event with Sadiya Hartman, Dionne Brand, Christina Sharpe, Torkwase Dyson, Canisia Lubrin, Kevin Adonis Browne, Dele Adeyemo, and Danai Mupotsa, hosted by The Sojourner Project on April 30, 2021.

THE CITY STRETCHES
In *Expulsions*, Saskia Sassen writes, "The city is eating vast stretches of dead land" (149) and about "pregnant pools" (160).

YOU TURN OFF YOUR LOCATION
This poem draws from Kerry Howley's article "Call Me a Traitor" in *Intelligencer* (specifically the line "It was hard to turn off the location data on your phone, and even if you made the effort, many apps would continue tracking, so most of us did

not bother."); the show *Succession* (particularly the reference to the wristwatch and the line "every time you look at it, it tells you exactly how rich you are" in episode 1 of season 1); and the tagline from an ad for Patek Philippe wristwatches: "You never actually own a Patek Philippe. You merely look after it for the next generation" (Nass, 2016).

TO THE END OF REDACTION
This poem draws from Daniel Estrin's article "Vaccines For Data: Israel's Pfizer Deal Drives Quick Rollout — And Privacy Worries?" on *NPR*.

TO THE END OF SENTIENCE
The framing of gangrene, decadence, and sickness comes from Aimé Césaire's *Discourse on Colonialism*. Dionne Brand in a conversation with Rinaldo Walcott at the 2020 R.W.B. Jackson Lecture says, "You live in whiteness without understanding it; there is so much you cannot imagine."

IN THE ALWAYS SAFETY OF THE CITY
In *Liquid Fear*, Zygmunt Bauman refers to "bunker language" and writes, "the English word 'safety' (absent, by the way, from many other European languages) mostly evokes the *personal*—material, bodily—aspects of security" (138). In a *Globe and Mail* interview in 2017, Dionne Brand states, "I've felt in my work, my poems and novels, the odd sensation of writing the city into being, though that city that I imagine, and that city that is possible, is yet unfinished."

A FINAL EPISODE
Return again to Dionne Brand: "that city that is possible, is yet unfinished."

Adnan, Etel. *Of Cities and Women*. The Post-Apollo Press, 1993.

Alsalaman, Yassin. *Text Messages: Or How I Found Myself Time Traveling*. Halifax, Roseway Publishing, 2020.

Althusser, Louis. *On the Reproduction of Capitalism*. London, Verso Books, 2014.

Apple. "Introducing Apple Vision Pro," 2023. https://www.youtube.com/watch?v=TX9qSaGXFyg

Bauman, Zygmunt. *Liquid Fear*. Cambridge, Polity Press, 2006.

Bauman, Zygmunt. *Liquid Love*. Cambridge, Polity Press, 2003.

Bauman, Zygmunt. *Liquid Modernity*. Cambridge, Polity Press, 2000.

Benjamin, Walter. "The Translator's Task." *The Translation Studies Reader*, translated by Steven Rendall, edited by Lawrence Venuti, New York, Routledge, 2021, pp. 89-97.

Benjamin, Walter. *Understanding Brecht*, translated by Anna Bostock, Brooklyn, NY, Verso Press, 2003.

Benjamin, Walter. "The Work of Art in the Age of Mechanical Reproduction." *Illuminations*, translated by Harry Zohn, edited by Hannah Arendt, New York, Harcourt Brace Jovanovich, 1968, pp. 217-53.

B-e, Lindsay. *The Cyborg Anthology*. Kingston, Brick Books, 2020.

Borzutzky, Daniel. *Lake Michigan*. University of Pittsburgh, 2018.

Brand, Dionne. "Dionne Brand: Nomenclature — New and Collected Poems," *Between the Covers Podcast*, 2023. https://tinhouse.com/podcast/dionne-brand-nomenclature-new-and-collected-poems/

Brand, Dionne. "2020 R.W.B. Jackson Lecture: Dionne Brand and Rinaldo Walcott," OISE, December 17, 2020.

Brand, Dionne. *The Blue Clerk*. Toronto, McClelland & Stewart, 2018.

Brand, Dionne. "The Shape of Language." Graham Foundation, 2018. https://www.youtube.com/watch?v=r_HdOZIFElo

Brand, Dionne. "Writing Against Tyranny and Toward Liberation," Barnard Center for Research on Women, April 25, 2017.

Brand, Dionne. "An Ars Poetica from *The Blue Clerk*." *The Black Scholar*, vol. 47, no. 1, 2017, pp. 58-77.

Brand, Dionne. *Ossuaries*. Toronto, McClelland & Stewart, 2010.

Brand, Dionne. *Inventory*. Toronto, McClelland & Stewart, 2006.

Brecht, Bertolt. "To Those Born Later." *The Collected Poems of Bertolt Brecht*, translated and edited by Tom Huhn and David Constantine, New York, W.W. Norton, 2015, pp. 734-736.

Brecht, Bertolt. "Five Difficulties on Writing Truth." *Brecht on Art and Politics*, edited by Steve Giles and Tom Kuhn, London, Bloomsbury, 2003.

Calvino, Italo. *Invisible Cities*. Boston, Mariner Books, 1972.

"Catastrophe :: Cartography" an event with Sadiya Hartman, Dionne Brand, Christina Sharpe, Torkwase Dyson, Canisia Lubrin, Kevin Adonis Browne, Dele Adeyemo, and Danai Mupotsa, hosted by The Sojourner Project on April 30, 2021. https://www.youtube.com/watch?v=HBLhkb8Qcaw

"Celebration." *Succession*, created by Jesse Armstrong, season 1, episode 1, Warner Bros. Television Distribution, 2018.

Césaire, Aimé. *Discourse on Colonialism*. New York, Monthly Review Press, 2021.

Césaire, Aimé. *Notebook of a Return to the Native Land*, translated by Clayton Eshleman and A. James Arnold, Wesleyan University Press, 2013.

Césaire, Aimé. *Notebook of a Return to the Native Land*, translated by Clayton Eshleman and Annette Smith, Wesleyan University Press, 2001.

Chakelian, Anoosh. "Capitalism's Over: The Man Who Made Millions by Betting the Economy Would Never Recover." *The New Statesman*, November 17, 2021.

Chamberlain, Joseph. "Mr. Chamberlain at Birmingham." *The Times*, January 6, 1885.

Chaya, Lynn. "Woman Groped by Stranger on Meta's Virtual Reality Social Media Platform." *National Post*, December 23, 2021.

Choi, Don Mee. *DMZ Colony*. Seattle, Wave Books, 2020.

Choi, Don Mee. *Translation is a Mode=Translation is an Antineocolonial Mode*. Inpress Books, 2020.

Choi, Franny. *Soft Science*. Farmington, ME, Alice James Books, 2019.

Chomsky, Noam. *Language and Mind*. Harcourt Brace Jovanovich, 1972.

Clarke, John. "Capitalism." *New Key Words: A Revised Vocabulary of Culture and Society*, edited by Tony Bennett, Lawrence Grossberg, and Meaghan Morris, Hoboken, NY, John Wiley & Sons, 2013, pp. 22-26.

Cronin, Michael. "The Translation Age: Translation, Technology, and the New Instrumentalism." *The Translation Reader*, 3rd ed., edited by Lawrence Venuti, New York, Routledge, 2012, pp. 469-482.

Davis, Wade. "The Unraveling of America." *Rolling Stone*, August 6, 2020.

di Prima, Diane. *Revolutionary Letters*. San Francisco, City Lights Books, 1979.

Diaz, Natalie. *Postcolonial Love Poem*. Minneapolis, MN, Graywolf Press, 2021.

Du Bois, W. E. B. "The Comet." *Darkwater: Voices from Within the Veil*. Mineola, NY, Dover Publication, 1999.

Dubord, Guy. *Society of the Spectacle*. Black & Red, 1970.

Estrin, Daniel. "Vaccines For Data: Israel's Pfizer Deal Drives Quick Rollout—And Privacy Worries?" *NPR*, January 31, 2021.

Fanon, Frantz. *The Wretched of the Earth*. London, Penguin, 1961.

Fred Again.., "Kyle (i found you)," https://www.npr.org/2023/04/10/1167158933/fred-again-tiny-desk-concert

Foucault, Michel. *Security, Territory, Population: Lectures at the College de France, 1977-1978*. New York, Palgrave Macmillan, 2004.

Georgiou, Aristos. "Scientists Consider Creating Magnetic Field Around Mars so We Can Colonize the Red Planet." *Newsweek*, November 22, 2021.

Gibson, Chantal. *How She Read*. Qualicum Beach, BC, Caitlin Press, 2020.

Gladman, Renee. *Event Factory*. St. Louis, MO, Dorothy, 2010.

Globe and Mail, The. "Order of Canada Honorees Desire a Better Country," June 30, 2017.

Graham, Laurie. D. *Fast Commute*. Toronto, McClelland & Stewart, 2022.

Gramsci, Antonio. *Selections from the Prison Notebooks*. International Publishers, 1971.

Great Hack, The. Produced and directed by Karim Amer and Jehane Noujaim. Netflix, 2019.

Hall, Stuart. *Policing the Crisis*. The Macmillan Press, 1978.

Hardt, Michael, and Antonio Negri. *Empire*. Harvard University Press, 2000.

Hill Collins, Patricia. "Preface: On Translation and Intellectual Activism." *Feminist Translation Studies: Local and Trans-national Perspectives*, edited by Olga Castro and Emek Ergun, Routledge, 2017, pp. xi-xvi.

Howley, Kerry. "Call Me a Traitor." *Intelligencer*, July 20, 2021.

Hughes, Langston. "My Adventures as a Social Poet." *Phylon* (1940-1956), vol. 8, no. 3 (3rd Qtr., 1947), pp. 205-212.

Hurston, Zora Neale. *Their Eyes Were Watching God*. J. B. Lippincott, 1937.

Hyesoon, Kim. *Autobiography of Death*. New York, New Directions, 2016.

Irwin, Neil. "The Pandemic Is Showing Us How Capitalism Is Amazing and Inadequate." *New York Times*, November 14, 2020.

Jones, Steve. "Virtual." *New Key Words: A Revised Vocabulary of Culture and Society*, edited by Tony Bennett, Lawrence Grossberg, and Meaghan Morris, Hoboken, NY, John Wiley & Sons, 2013, pp. 367-369.

Kim, Tae. "Goldman Sachs Asks in Biotech Research Report: 'Is Curing Patients a Sustainable Business Model?'" *CNBC*, April 11, 2018.

Lai, Larissa. *Automaton Biographies*. Vancouver, BC, Arsenal Press, 2009.

Lorde, Audre. *Sister Outsider: Essays and Speeches*. Freedom, CA, Crossing Press, 1984.

Lorenz, Taylor. "Birds Aren't Real, or Are They? Inside a Gen Z Conspiracy Theory." *New York Times*, December 9, 2021.

Lubrin, Canisia. *The Dyzgraphxst*. Toronto, McClelland & Stewart, 2020.

Manchester Guardian, The. Miscellany, Quote by William Morris. Page 5, Columns 3 and 4, Manchester, England, June 6, 1921.

Maracle, Lee. *I Am Woman: A Native Perspective on Sociology and Feminism*. Press Gang Publishers, 1988.

Mayer, Bernadette. *Sonnets*. Tender Buttons Press, 2014.

Micallef, Shawn. "Toronto Shows Its Ugly, Brutish Side in Clearing of Trinity Bellwoods Encampment." *The Toronto Star*, June 23, 2021.

Miliband, Ralph. *The State in Capitalist Society*. Merlin Press, 2009.

Mitchell, W. T. J. "Value." *New Key Words: A Revised Vocabulary of Culture and Society*, edited by Tony Bennett, Lawrence Grossberg, and Meaghan Morris, Hoboken, NY, John Wiley & Sons, 2013, pp. 365-367.

Monáe, Janelle. "Pynk." *Dirty Computer*. Wondaland, 2018.

Morley, David. "Media." *New Key Words: A Revised Vocabulary of Culture and Society*, edited by Tony Bennett, Lawrence Grossberg, and Meaghan Morris, Hoboken, NY, John Wiley & Sons, 2013, pp. 211-214.

Moure, Erín. *Pillage Laud*. BookThug, 1999.

Nass, Roberta. "Patek Phillipe Celebrates 20 Years of Its Iconic Advertising Campaign." *Forbes*, December 9, 2016.

Neruda, Pablo. "Letter to Miguel Otero Silva, in Caracas." *Windows that Open Inward: Images of Chili*. Buffalo, NY, White Pine Press, 1985.

Nietzsche, Friedrich. "Translations." *The Translation Studies Reader*, 4th ed., translated by Walter Kaufmann, edited by Lawrence Venuti, New York, Routledge, 2012, pp. 75-76.

Ogawa, Yōko. *The Memory Police*. New York, Pantheon, 2019.

Perrigo, Billy. "Exclusive: OpenAI Used Kenyan Workers on Less Than $2 Per Hour to Make ChatGPT Less Toxic." *TIME*, January 18, 2023.

Peters, Sara. "Rehearsal." *1996*. Toronto, House of Anansi Press, 2013.

Porter, Catherine. "The Carpenter Who Built Tiny Homes for Toronto's Homeless." *New York Times*, April 16, 2021.

Prasad, Vijay. "What is the Meaning of the Left?" *Global Radicalism: Solidarity, Internationalism, and Feminist Futures*, November 16, 2018.

Preciado, Paul B. "Learning from the Virus." *ArtForum*, May/June 2020.

Rafael, Vincente L. "Translation, American English, and the National Insecurities of Empire." *The Translation Reader*, 4th ed., edited by Lawrence Venuti, New York, Routledge, 2021, pp. 436-452.

Rankine, Claudia. *Citizen: An American Lyric*. Minneapolis, MN, Graywolf Press, 2014.

Rankine, Claudia. *Don't Let Me Be Lonely: An American Lyric*. Minneapolis, MN, Graywolf Press, 2004.

Rich, Adrienne. *The Dream of a Common Language*. New York, W. W. Norton & Co., 1993.

Rich, Adrienne. *An Atlas of the Difficult World*. New York, W. W. Norton & Co., 1991.

Rich, Adrienne. *Diving in the Wreck: Poems 1971-1972*. New York, W. W. Norton & Co., 1973.

Robin, Raizel. "The $1-Billion Hellhole." *Toronto Life*, February 15, 2017.

Rodrick, Stephen. "Jeremy Strong on Succession, The Trial of The Chicago 7." *Rolling Stone* [interview], October 15, 2020.

Roubaud, Jacques. *The Form of a City Changes Faster, Alas, Than the Human Heart*, translated by Keith Waldrop and Rosmarie Waldrop. London, Dalkey Press, 2006.

Roy, Arundhati. "Come September." *The End of Imagination*. Chicago, Haymarket Books, 2016, pp. 237-252.

Rukeyser, Muriel. *The Book of the Dead*. West Virginia University Press, 2018.

Said, Edward. *Culture and Imperialism*. New York, Vintage Books, 1994.

Salas Rivera, Raquel. *while they sleep (under the bed is another country)*. Minneapolis, MN, Birds, LLC, 2017.

Salazar, Rebecca. *sulphurtongue*. Toronto, McClelland & Stewart, 2021.

Sassen, Saskia. *Expulsions*. Cambridge, MA, The Belknap Press of Harvard University Press, 2014.

Sassen, Saskia. "When the City Itself Becomes a Technology of War." *Theory, Culture, & Society*, vol. 27, no. 6, December 17, 2010, pp. 33-50.

Seven Prisoners. Directed by Alexandre Moratto, Netflix, 2021.

Sharif, Solmaz. *Look*. Minneapolis, MN, Graywolf Press, 2016.

Sharpe, Christina. *Ordinary Notes*. Knopf Canada, 2023.

Sharpe, Christina. Biennale Arte 2022, Meetings on Art: What Could A Vessel Be?, June 11, 2022. https://www.youtube.com/watch?v=4BYPvgRJGQg

Simone, Nina. *Wild Is the Wind*. Philips Records, 1966.

Simpson, Leanne Betasamosake. *Noopiming: The Cure for White Ladies*. Toronto, House of Anansi Press, 2020.

Smalley, Eric. "How Vulnerable Is Your Personal Information? 4 Essential Reads." *The Conversation*, November 29, 2021.

Smith, Dorothy E. *The Everyday World as Problematic: A Feminist Sociology*. University of Toronto Press, 1987.

Spivak, Gayatri Chakravorty. "The Politics of Translation." *The Translation Reader*, 4th ed., edited by Lawrence Venuti, New York, Routledge, 2021, pp. 320-338.

Spivak, Gayatri Chakravorty. "Gayatri Spivak's Lecture— Necessary & Impossible: Culture as Translation," ILF Samanway Translations Series, April 9, 2018.

"Statue of Egerton Ryerson, Toppled after Toronto Rally, 'Will Not Be Restored or Replaced,'" *CBC News*, June 6, 2021.

Thiong'o, Ngũgĩ wa. "The Politics of Translation." *The Language of Languages: Reflections on Translation*. Seagull Books, 2023.

Turner, Bryan. "Citizenship." *New Key Words: A Revised Vocabulary of Culture and Society*, edited by Tony Bennett, Lawrence Grossberg, and Meaghan Morris, Hoboken, NY, John Wiley & Sons, 2013, pp. 29-32.

Van Clief-Stefanon, Lyrae. "Bop: The North Star." *Open Interval*. University of Pittsburgh Press, 2009.

VanderKlippe, Nathan. "No Place to Hide: An Artistic Exploration of Urban Surveillance Cameras on Beijing Streets," *The Globe and Mail*, November 1, 2020.

Walcott, Derek. "Map of the New World." *Collected Poems 1948-1984*. Farrar, Straus & Giroux, LLC, 1986.

Wang, Phoebe. *Waking Occupations*. Toronto, McClelland & Stewart, 2022.

Wang, Phoebe. *Admission Requirements*. Toronto, McClelland & Stewart, 2017.

Williams, Raymond. *The Country and the City*. Chatto and Windus, 1973.

Wong, Rita. *forage*. Gibson's Landing, BC, Nightwood Editions, 2008.

Wright, C.D. *Rising, Falling, Hovering*. Washington, Copper Canyon Press, 2009.

Zuboff, Shoshana. *Shoshana Zuboff on Surveillance Capitalism*. Directed by Roland Duong, VPRO Documentary, 2019.

Zurita, Raúl. *Song for His Disappeared Love*. Notre Dame, IN, ActionBooks, 2010.

Zurita, Raúl. "Today or a Million Years Ago: An Interview with Raúl Zurita. An interview by Daniel Borzutzky." *Poetry Foundation*, 2014.

ANNA LEE-POPHAM is a writer and editor who has published poetry and non-fiction in *Arc Poetry Magazine, Brick, Canthius, Riddle Fence, Autostraddle, Lingue e Linguaggi*, and others. Anna holds an MFA in Creative Writing from the University of Guelph and lives in Toronto.